BEAUTY **SECRETS** **of** Transgender Bombshells

This book is dedicated to my fur baby, Snuggles.

He passed away on August 28, 2022.

Thank you for giving me 15 years and 3 months of unconditional love.

I will always love you…

A book by Amanda Valentine

G000138143

Table of Contents

Dedication

Being a transgender woman not only provided me with a wider perspective. It also opened my eyes to a smorgasbord of beauty.

But out of all the transgender women I've met and cultivated friendships with, I'm still in awe of one kind of transgender woman.

She's the kind that can make a man risk everything.

The type that can't walk ten steps without being seen.

Her irresistible beauty defies societal norms and sexual orientations.

She is the Transgender Bombshell.

I dedicate this book to transgender bombshells all over the world who are using their beauty to elevate trans women's image.

Foreword

We all have a bombshell within us. Some just don't know how to unleash it yet.

Transgender women are like witches. We have the power to put men under our spell if we choose to do so.

If you haven't discovered your feminine power yet, I'm here to help you.

With many years of physically transitioning, I've learned many beauty secrets from transgender bombshells.

Their impeccable beauty maintenance routines, eye for style, and natural knowledge of seduction are all going to be revealed in this intimate tgirl-to-tgirl talk.

Tip 1 - Bombshell Beauty Routine

Every bombshell has a beauty routine. Any hot tgirl who says that she barely does anything is lying to you. Remember, we're not talking about girl-next-doors.

We're talking about BOMBSHELLS

In this section, I'm going to be very in-depth. So much so that we'll be talking about their beauty routine not only from head to toe but from scalp to soles.

Crowning Glory

A boring bun and a work-out ponytail won't cut it. Bombshells have big, long, and healthy hair.

Men are naturally attracted to women who possess these types of locks. Not only because this kind of hair is universally glorified, but it also has something to do with men's genetic code.

If you want to be the center of men's attention, you need to learn how to style your hair and take care of it.

It must be long, shiny, voluminous, and bouncy!

Google Barbara Mori when she played Rubi. Her hair in the show is the perfect example of what men want.

Bombshell Makeup

Ditch the current makeup trend of making everyone look like a shiny caterpillar.

Too much highlight and moisturizer will make you look sweaty.

Moreover, stop trying to achieve the bushy brows look.

It looks great in photos but it doesn't translate well in person.

Don't mistake the bombshell look for the street hooker mug.

Bombshells, albeit possessing a sexy image, don't look unkempt, wet, and wild.

Their makeup is fresh, immaculate, and sexy.

You can take inspiration from how Marilyn Monroe did her makeup.

It's the perfect combo of the ever-feminine arched eyebrows and the kiss-commanding red lips.

Skin, Teeth, and Nails

As discussed earlier, bombshells are fresh. They must be because not a lot of men will fantasize about sleeping with a dirty-looking transgender woman.

Pay attention to your skin. Bombshells are flawless. Their presence won't be as commanding if they don't have clean and moisturized skin.

Don't skip your dental appointments and never neglect your teeth.

Bombshells spend a lot on their upkeep and they don't skimp on this area.

Bad teeth give off an image of bad breath. Who would want to kiss you if you give off this vibe?

Finally, nails are telling if a transgender woman takes good care of herself.

If your nails are not clean and painted, you're going to miss out on a lot of men.

Hundreds of surveys have been made and most men prefer manicured nails.

They find them sexy!

Tip 2 – Red is Power

Every bombshell knows the power of the color red.

Psychologically, men think of sex when they see this color.

If you're not going to capitalize on it, you'll have a harder time being a bombshell.

Red can be used in many ways. You can take it slow by incorporating it subtly.

Some only wear it on their lips and in most cases, that's sufficient enough.

Others love wearing accessories such as red shoes and handbags.

Now, if you really want to be the star of the show, you can never go wrong with a red dress.

The song *Lady in Red* is not popular for no reason!

However, like any other power, you must know how to properly wield it.

Don't wear red from head to toe. You're going to look like a mascot.

Before filling out your wardrobe with this color, you must also know that not all shades of red may work for your skin tone.

Color theorists have published studies that there's the perfect shade of red for everyone.

You must know whether you're warm or cool-toned to truly know which type of red suits you best.

Now, if you turn out to have a neutral skin tone, thank your lucky stars.

You can add all kinds of red to your cart without any issues.

Tip 3 - They Often Come in Twos

A bombshell must learn how to look busy and uninterested.

Her sexy status will die as soon as she appears desperate.

However, you must know that this tip is only required if you're going to a special event or a bar.

You don't need to bring your partner and the whole posse with you at all times.

Find someone who shares the same values and create the perfect clubbing bombshell duo.

Take it from Paris Hilton. In her it-girl days in the early 2000s, she was never seen clubbing alone.

She usually had equally hot girlfriends with her.

Nothing's as sad as the sight of a scantily-dressed transgender woman alone in a bar.

It gives off an image that she's looking for a John.

Men should see you having fun with your friends and looking busy.

He will find it more challenging to talk to you and fuel his fire to want you more.

From this day forward, start cultivating friendships.

Don't worry if you think that your friend is hotter than you. You're both hot. It's not a competition.

Clubbing with girlfriends is more of teamwork than a game of who's going to get the most guys.

Men have different tastes so you'll get your share.

Tip 4 – The Bombshell Style

Forget the Barbie Doll, Emo, and Girl-next-door types of fashion.

None of those will work.

The Bombshell style is mature, sexy, and mysterious.

It's often form-fitting and provocative.

Bombshells enjoy wearing skirts, dresses, corsets, and tight pants.

They rarely wear short shorts because they're not going for the Hoochie Mama look.

Many of them can be seen wearing cowl-neck dresses and bold colors.

They also sometimes experiment with animal prints but they know how to use them sparingly.

If you want to get a clearer picture of a bombshell's style, feel free to look up Monica Bellucci fashion.

She is the epitome of how a classy bombshell dresses up.

Another tip to remember when dressing up is never show everything all at once.

If you're showing your cleavage, don't show too much leg.

Should you wear a backless dress, hide your other assets.

If your dress has a high slit, don't let the babies out.

A bombshell is sexy but she also knows that her body is not for free.

She has perfected the art of just showing enough to make a man's imagination run wild.

Tip 5 – She Knows How to Shut Up

How can you create a mysteriously sexy image if your voice sounds like a machine gun?

A bombshell creates mystery by having a serene yet strong persona.

If you keep talking over a man, he will find you comical.

Your bombshell look won't matter so much because he knows that you're just playing dress-up.

A true bombshell has a sexy appearance but possesses a soft demeanor.

You don't have to impress a man. That's not your job as a transgender woman.

You don't have to prove that you're smart by talking too much. Remember, emotional intelligence matters as well and if you don't know how to read social cues, you will appear dumb.

The best way to mitigate men being turned off is by knowing how to shut up.

Again, it is the man's job most especially in the early stages to impress you.

Let him do all the talking and just enjoy how powerful your femininity is.

Compare Samantha Jones with Carrie Bradshaw, the reason why the latter is not the bombshell in the hit TV show Sex and the City is that she talks too much.

Samantha is a woman of few words but every word she utters is impactful.

This is the reason why it's easier for her to attract men.

She knows when her mouth is needed.

Tip 6 – Her Scent

Apart from the exorbitant dental fees, bombshells also invest in high-quality fragrances.

They don't just use anything that's in the drugstore aisle.

Bombshells often avoid perfumes that are too sweet and fruity because those scents do not represent who they are.

They go for something more striking and sexy.

Most of them also prefer Eau de Parfums because they want something that'll last the whole day.

Because they're bombshells, it's not hard for them to end up in proximity to a man.

That's why they always ensure that their scent will positively linger in men's brains.

Some good examples of flirty yet not too mature high-quality scents are Coco Mademoiselle by Chanel and Rose N'Roses by Dior.

Based on my experience, many transgender bombshells that I know own a bottle of Versace Bright Crystal. It's pretty safe yet still bombshell-worthy.

Tip 7 – A Bombshell's Demeanor

Her strides and glides are quite feminine. She's swaying her hips when she walks but doesn't overdo it.

Whenever she picks up things and creates other gestures, she does so with grace and softness.

You'll also hardly see her look like hustled. There's a reason why the saying "It's better to be late than arrive ugly" is so popular.

If you always look like you're in a hurry and you're talking at a rate of 50 words per minute, your mojo will die.

You're not only going to look silly, but you'll also look like you're high on something.

Moreover, also pay close attention to how you ride a car, sit, and stand.

Avoid fidgeting and odd-looking twitches like the constant fixing of the hair.

Always stop your urge of retouching your makeup in public. You had plenty of time to perfect it at home. It shouldn't curtail you from propelling to becoming a transgender bombshell.

Ditch bubblegums most especially if you're in your full bombshell attire. You're going to look like a stereotypical street walker.

Lastly, when you're alone in a restaurant, avoid spinning your head in a 360-degree motion. Not that you can do that but you get the gist.

When you're sitting down, avoid looking in all directions. This will make you look desperate.

Try to occupy yourself with either your phone, the menu, or a book.

Tip 8 – Sexy Shoes

Every bombshell owns a pair of sexy stilettoes.

If your shoe rack is filled with nothing but flats and sneakers, it's time to do some shopping.

Yes, wearing sexy shoes often hurt but there's always a price to beauty.

Moreover, there are high heels that were made for walking. You just have to find them.

Of course, I'm not going to torture you by not telling you how to do so.

But you definitely won't find them online!

The secret to ensuring that your sexy shoes are walkable is by buying them in physical stores.

Try them on for more than thirty minutes and if they don't pinch your feet too much, buy them!

Here's a helpful tip, if you have wide feet, try looking for round-toe heels.

While pointy ones are sexier, they're not that bad and they're more forgiving.

Added to that, anything that's less than four inches can't be considered a transgender bombshell shoe.

That's for running errands or working out.

Enjoy being feminine. Have a Mariah Carey working out while wearing high heels in MTV Cribs moment.

Tip 9 – Love for Lingerie

Lastly, no self-respecting transgender bombshell will wear granny undies most especially if she's out and about.

To them, lingerie is like a second skin.

Added to that, because you're a maneater, you must always be prepared for surprise moments.

Not that I'm telling you to sleep with every guy you attract but you know what I mean.

Always make sure that your lingerie pieces match. You'll look like an 80s superhero with mismatched underwear.

There's no strict rule on what style and fabric your lingerie should be.

But silk, lace, and leather are always effective in making a man desire you more.

Bonus – What they All Wear

Now that you know how to be a bombshell, the last form of garment that's necessary to complete your look is not tangible.

Can you make a guess?

Ding ding ding! You got that right, CONFIDENCE!

Being a transgender bombshell requires a lot so it's only right for you to be confident.

After all of these efforts, you should have no reason to be insecure anymore.

I didn't include how your body should look because from my experiences, transgender bombshells come in all forms.

Whether you're a skinny mini or a plus size, men will find you irresistible if you flawlessly wear confidence.

Remember, not all men fall for the stereotypical idea of beauty.

You can create your own market just by acknowledging that you're one hot transgender bombshell!

Now strut your stuff and go forth. Use everything you've learned from here and transform into the woman you're meant to be!

Author's Message

Dear Ladies,

Thank you very much for purchasing and reading Beauty Secrets of Transgender Bombshells.

For a writer, I can't seem to find the best word to describe how grateful I am for your support.

If you enjoyed this book, kindly give it a rating on Kindle.

Let's get it to the overall bestseller list <3

Should you feel the need to send me a message concerning this book, your love life, or just about anything, please feel free to follow the pages below and subscribe to my mailing list to get updates on new releases.

Homepage (www.dtwfgbook.com)

Facebook (DTWFG Community)

Twitter (Personal Account)

My Transgender Date Column (My Latest Articles)

She knows when, where, and how to wield them. Even if she's dressed up casually, her elegance emanates effortlessly. The power that she holds goes beyond grabbing attention.

She is The Classy Transgender Lady.

In this book, Amanda Valentine is going to teach you everything about her.

You have everything that it takes. You just need to read the manual.

Elevate your image and achieve everything you desire in life with these simple yet helpful tips.

Get a Copy – mybook.to/tctlbook

Dating Transgender Women for Gentlemen is **a collection of trans women's real experiences in the ever-punishing world we all call online dating**.

Let Amanda Valentine's 13 years of bad romance tell you what trans women truly want in a life partner.

Get a Copy – www.dtwfgbook.com

Cover Vector Designed by: vektorpocket from Freepik